STICKMEN'S GUIDE TO GIGANTIC MACHINES

by John Farndon
Illustrated by John Paul

HUNGRY
TOMATO™

Germany's bucket wheel excavator is almost as long as 2.5 football pitches.

Contents

Gigantic Machines

You are completely surrounded by machines. Scissors, computers, central-heating systems, screwdrivers, door handles, bicycles and countless other things are all machines. Most of these are human-sized. But the machines in this book are truly monstrous. They're all made by humans, of course, but they are so big they seem like the machines of giants.

The factory machine

The biggest machines in the world are actually factories. Some factories need quite a lot of help from workers to make things. But in many of the largest car factories, more and more of the work is done by robots. Modern car factories, such as BMW's in Munich, are like scenes from *Transformers*, with robot arms whirling relentlessly as they put together car after car.

The world's smallest machines

The machines in this book are awesomely big. But there are now machines that are just as awesomely tiny. They are called nanomachines, and are so small you can see them only under the most powerful electron microscopes. One team at Rice University in Texas, USA, made a car no bigger than a molecule. But perhaps the most exciting are the nanorobot doctors being developed. They can be injected into your bloodstream to investigate and repair damage, or even deliver drugs on target.

Mystery stone movers

All over the world, prehistoric people have left behind giant stones called megaliths. The biggest underpin an ancient temple at Baalbek in Lebanon. They weigh up to 1,600 tons each, and no one knows how they were moved from the quarry 800 m (½ mile) away. French archaeologist Jean-Pierre Adam thinks it was with machines that we now know nothing about, involving rollers, winding cables and pulleys.

Big pit

Some of the biggest machines in this book are diggers, designed to excavate pits like the enormous Bingham Canyon copper mine near Salt Lake City in Utah, USA. Machines dig out nearly half a million tons of rock here every day, and have made a hole 4.4 km (2¾ miles) across and 1.2 km (¾ mile) deep. If this were a basketball stadium, it would have room for every single person in New York City, and a few more.

The farthest machines

No machines are farther away than Voyagers 1 and 2. These space probes, launched in 1977, have been heading out into space ever since. Voyager 1 is 12 billion miles away and Voyager 2 10 billion miles away – and they are getting hundreds of miles farther away every second. Voyager 1 zoomed entirely out of the solar system in 2012.

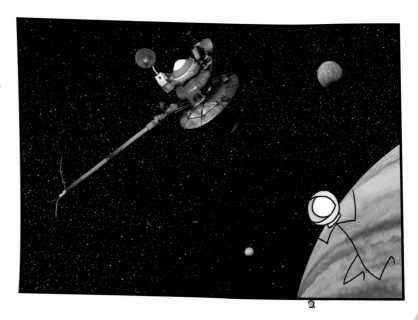

History of Gigantic Machines

The story of enormous machines goes farther back in time than you might imagine. Many of the biggest machines have been built since the Industrial Revolution two centuries or so ago. But some extraordinary machines existed in the ancient world, too – in Ancient Egypt, Greece, Rome and China.

340BCE
Ancient Greek engineer Polydus of Thessaly invented Helepolis, the biggest siege machine ever: a 40-m (130-ft), armour-plated tower on wheels designed to attack city walls. It got stuck in the mud.

1st century CE
The Roman Barbegal mills in France used a staircase of 16 giant waterwheels to grind huge quantities of wheat (4.5 tons a day) into flour. A big round for the Romans!

2000BCE   1300BCE   600BCE   200BCE

3000BCE
The Ancient Egyptians developed the ramp to build their gigantic stone pyramids. The work was inclined to be hard.

214BCE
Scientist and inventor Archimedes of Syracuse in Sicily created a giant crane with an iron claw. It ripped attacking Roman ships from the water. Things picked up for the Syracusans.

12th century

Kurdish military engineer Mardi ibn Ali al-Tarsusi wrote about giant counterweight trebuchets – catapult machines that could sling missiles as big as a car at the enemy. They had it coming.

1839

American William Otis (cousin of lift inventor Elisha Otis) invented the steam shovel, the grandaddy of all mechanical excavators. It got him into a big hole.

1907

The Titan Crane was erected in Clydebank, UK, to help build ships such as the *Queen Elizabeth*. At the time, it was the world's largest cantilever or 'hammerhead' crane and the first electric crane. It could lift 160 tons (equivalent to 26 African elephants).

50CE   650CE   1200   2000

1780

Boat lifts capable of lifting entire canal boats from one canal level to another were invented. The oldest preserved example is the Anderton boat lift in Cheshire, UK, dating from 1875. Today, the world's biggest, just opened at the Three Gorges Dam in China, can lift entire ships!

1913

Henry Ford created the first car assembly line to make Model T Ford cars in large numbers – and the first traffic jams.

1825

British engineer Marc Isambard Brunel invented the tunnel boring machine to create a tunnel under the River Thames. Only the mud got bored.

Dump Trucks

Mining companies need huge quantities of rocks moved fast – and the best way to do this is with giant dump trucks, sometimes called haul trucks. These big-as-a-house mine monsters never have to go on the road, so there is no limit to size – the bigger the better. All that matters is moving loads of rubble, fast. But mines are very tough, too. So these trucks have to be super-tough.

The cab

The driver's cab is so small compared to the truck you can barely see it – and to reach it, the driver has to climb a ladder. The driver, of course, has power-assisted steering to steer those mighty wheels!

Turning tight

The truck has to make turns in tight places, so the front wheels can swivel a long way. That means a haul truck like the BelAZ 75710 can turn right round in its own length.

Brute force

The powerhouse of a haul truck has to be unstoppable. That's why trucks like the BelAZ 75710 have two engines, not one, and they are both 16-cylinder diesels. The engines are simply electricity generators which produce the electricity to drive hugely powerful electric motors on four of the wheels, turning them directly.

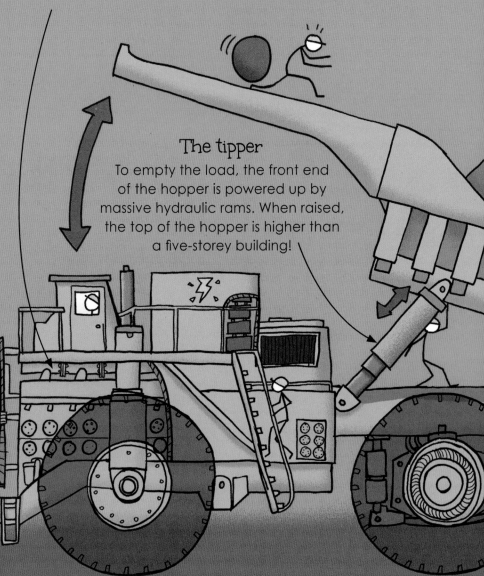

The tipper

To empty the load, the front end of the hopper is powered up by massive hydraulic rams. When raised, the top of the hopper is higher than a five-storey building!

Big digger

Haul trucks often get their load direct from another huge machine, a mechanical digger. This is like a giant spade that digs out the ground with a bucket moved by a hinged arm. The arm gets its power from hydraulic (fluid-filled) pistons. The digging arm and cabin are on a swivelling turntable, so it can be easily manoeuvred.

High and mighty

Right now, the biggest dump truck in the world is the BelAZ 75710 made in Belarus. It can move more than 450 tons of rubble in a single load. That's the weight of 250 or so cars, or 40 African elephants! To shift all that weight, it has an engine with a torque (turning force) of 13,738 lb–ft – about 24 times that of a 2014 Formula One racing car!

How much?

If you wanted to buy a BelAZ 75710, it would cost you a cool £3,940,000 ($6,000,000)…

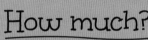

The hopper

The load is carried in the truck's hopper which is made from massively thick steel to take the weight and the constant battering of rubble. The hopper is filled up by mechanical diggers or an overhead conveyor. But it needs to be unloaded instantly. That's why the hopper is designed to tip up, so the load can slide straight out.

Big wheels

Monster dump trucks run on what may be the world's biggest wheels. They're typically taller than an African elephant – about the height of two tall adults put together. And there are usually six or eight of them – each with absolutely massive rubber tyres. Those tyres are supremely tough and chunky – you don't want a puncture with one of these!

Construction Cranes

Right now, scores of buildings more than 300 m (1,000 ft) tall are going up in cities all over the world. To build them, they need cranes that are just as tall – the tallest ever built. And these cranes don't just need to be tall. They have to lift very heavy weights and manoeuvre them to exactly where they are needed. This high up, even a small error could be disastrous.

Operator's cab

A crane operator's job is a tough one. You really need a head for heights. You have to be fit, too. Every morning you climb vertical ladders all the way up to the cab and, usually, drop in through the roof. Once inside, you'll be there all day – until you climb all the way back down again.

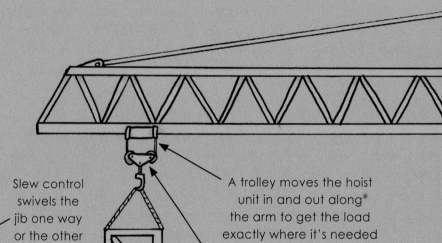

Slew control swivels the jib one way or the other

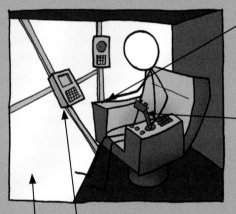

A trolley moves the hoist unit in and out along the arm to get the load exactly where it's needed

The hook that lifts the load is attached to the hoist unit

Hoist unit

Hoist control lever starts the hoist winding up or down

Computer screen shows the weight of the load, the climb speed, wind speed and much more

Electronic systems ensure the load and hoist speed are perfectly matched

Video systems give the operator a close-up view of the hook and load

The tallest ever

The world's tallest cranes are not at their full height yet. These are the Liebherr cranes being used to build what will be the world's tallest building: the Kingdom Tower (left) in Jeddah, Saudi Arabia. The biggest, used in constructing the central tower, is a 'climbing crane', which means it will extend as the building rises, using it as support. The last section of crane, for lifting the top of the building into place, will be over 1,000 m (3,280 ft) up! Yet it will still only be 2.4 m (8 ft) wide.

Windows are made of laminated safety glass

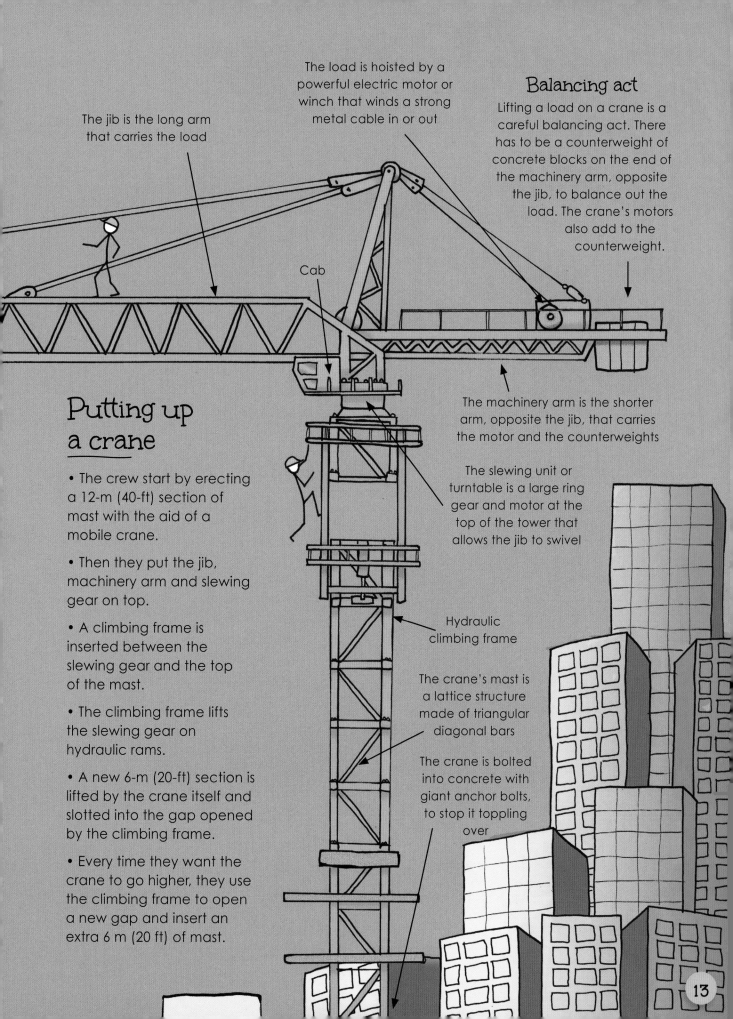

The load is hoisted by a powerful electric motor or winch that winds a strong metal cable in or out

The jib is the long arm that carries the load

Balancing act

Lifting a load on a crane is a careful balancing act. There has to be a counterweight of concrete blocks on the end of the machinery arm, opposite the jib, to balance out the load. The crane's motors also add to the counterweight.

Cab

The machinery arm is the shorter arm, opposite the jib, that carries the motor and the counterweights

The slewing unit or turntable is a large ring gear and motor at the top of the tower that allows the jib to swivel

Putting up a crane

• The crew start by erecting a 12-m (40-ft) section of mast with the aid of a mobile crane.

• Then they put the jib, machinery arm and slewing gear on top.

• A climbing frame is inserted between the slewing gear and the top of the mast.

• The climbing frame lifts the slewing gear on hydraulic rams.

• A new 6-m (20-ft) section is lifted by the crane itself and slotted into the gap opened by the climbing frame.

• Every time they want the crane to go higher, they use the climbing frame to open a new gap and insert an extra 6 m (20 ft) of mast.

Hydraulic climbing frame

The crane's mast is a lattice structure made of triangular diagonal bars

The crane is bolted into concrete with giant anchor bolts, to stop it toppling over

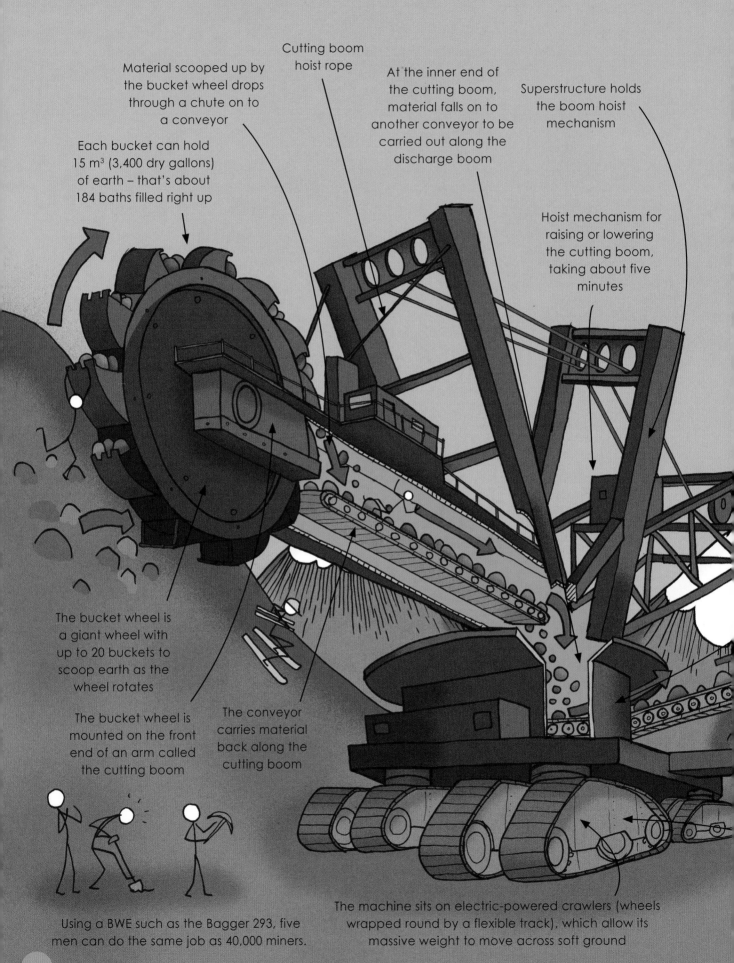

Material scooped up by the bucket wheel drops through a chute on to a conveyor

Cutting boom hoist rope

At the inner end of the cutting boom, material falls on to another conveyor to be carried out along the discharge boom

Superstructure holds the boom hoist mechanism

Each bucket can hold 15 m³ (3,400 dry gallons) of earth – that's about 184 baths filled right up

Hoist mechanism for raising or lowering the cutting boom, taking about five minutes

The bucket wheel is a giant wheel with up to 20 buckets to scoop earth as the wheel rotates

The bucket wheel is mounted on the front end of an arm called the cutting boom

The conveyor carries material back along the cutting boom

Using a BWE such as the Bagger 293, five men can do the same job as 40,000 miners.

The machine sits on electric-powered crawlers (wheels wrapped round by a flexible track), which allow its massive weight to move across soft ground

Bucket Wheel Excavators

Gigantic bucket wheel excavators (BWEs) are the world's most monstrous vehicles. With their whirling bucket wheels, they can chew through the ground at a furious rate. The biggest can shift hundreds of thousands of tons of ground material, carving a deep gouge in the earth.

Big Bagger

The biggest BWE, and the biggest vehicle ever, is the Bagger 293, which mines brown coal near Hambach in Germany. It's 225 m (738 ft) long and 96 m (315 ft) tall – much longer and almost as tall as St Paul's Cathedral in London. It also weighs a crushing 14,200 tons! And it's got wheels, or rather, crawlers.

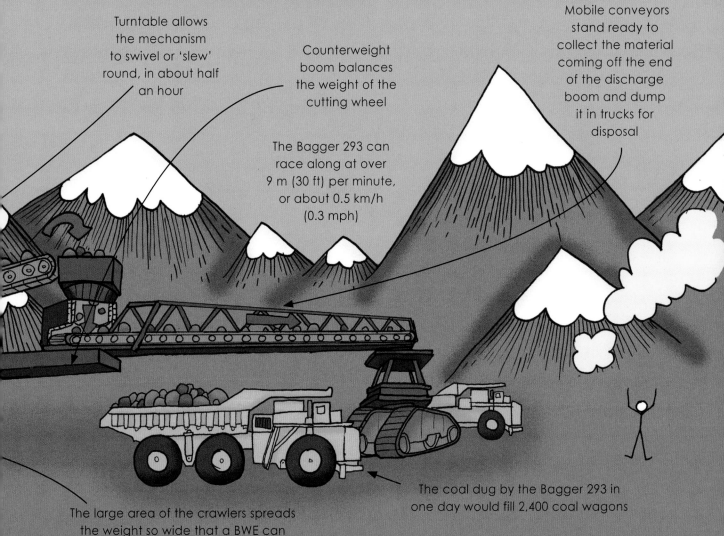

Turntable allows the mechanism to swivel or 'slew' round, in about half an hour

Counterweight boom balances the weight of the cutting wheel

Mobile conveyors stand ready to collect the material coming off the end of the discharge boom and dump it in trucks for disposal

The Bagger 293 can race along at over 9 m (30 ft) per minute, or about 0.5 km/h (0.3 mph)

The coal dug by the Bagger 293 in one day would fill 2,400 coal wagons

The large area of the crawlers spreads the weight so wide that a BWE can move over grass without damaging it

Tunnelling Machines

If you want to dig a really big tunnel, you need a boring machine – a tunnel boring machine or TBM. These are like gigantic drills that bore through the ground, leaving a complete tunnel behind them. Without them, city metro systems, mains water services, road and other tunnels could not have been built.

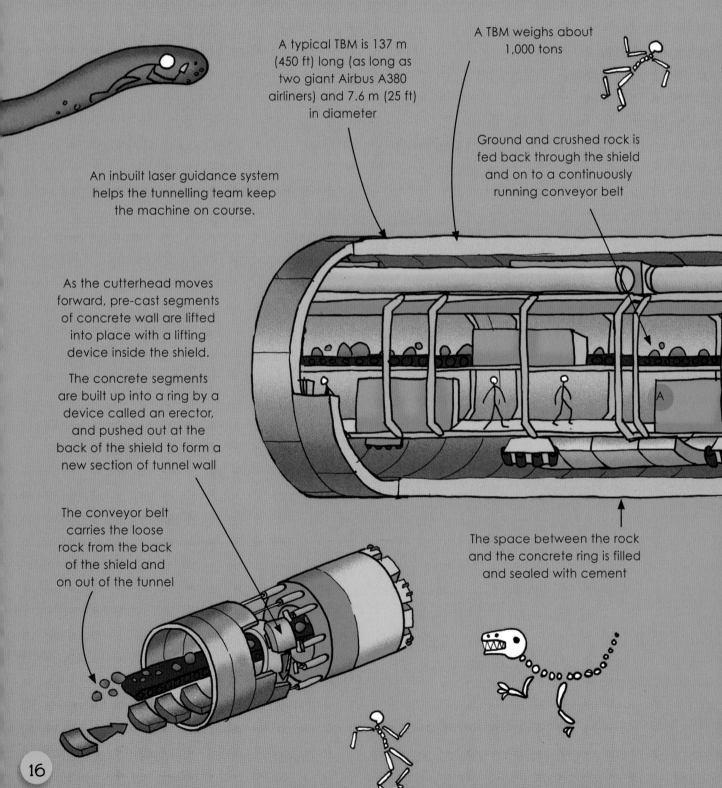

A typical TBM is 137 m (450 ft) long (as long as two giant Airbus A380 airliners) and 7.6 m (25 ft) in diameter

A TBM weighs about 1,000 tons

An inbuilt laser guidance system helps the tunnelling team keep the machine on course.

Ground and crushed rock is fed back through the shield and on to a continuously running conveyor belt

As the cutterhead moves forward, pre-cast segments of concrete wall are lifted into place with a lifting device inside the shield.

The concrete segments are built up into a ring by a device called an erector, and pushed out at the back of the shield to form a new section of tunnel wall

The conveyor belt carries the loose rock from the back of the shield and on out of the tunnel

The space between the rock and the concrete ring is filled and sealed with cement

The TBM needs only a small team and the operator controlling the cutterhead sits some way behind in a control booth, monitoring progress on screens fed by cameras at the head.

Workers' rest room

The electric and hydraulic power systems are way behind the cutter

Pressure sensors continually monitor the turning power of the cutterhead and adjustments are made automatically

The front of the TBM is a cylinder called a shield, because it shields the tunnellers as they dig

The cutterhead is driven round by powerful electric motors and grinds away the rock

Powerful hydraulic rams press the cutterhead up against the rockface

The front of the shield is a giant disc facing into the new rock. It's called the cutterhead and is fitted with incredibly tough steel cutting edges and scrapers

Big Bertha gets stuck

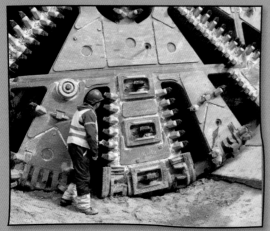

North America's biggest borer is Big Bertha, named after the USA's first female mayor, Bertha Knight Landes, who was mayor of Seattle in the 1920s. Big Bertha weighs 7,000 tons and has a cutterhead 17.5 m (57.5 ft) in diameter. In 2013, it began drilling a massive double-decker highway tunnel in Seattle, cutting through 9 m (30 ft) of solid rock every day. But after 300 m (1,000 ft), it ground to a halt as grit got into its bearings. Engineers took over a year to work out how to replace the bearings!

Combine Harvesters

When harvest time comes each year, wheat fields around the world begin to throb with the sound of giant machines called combine harvesters. Their task is to cut down the ripe wheat and gather the grain to make the flour we need for our bread. The world's biggest combine harvester, the Lexion 780, can gather over 700 tons of grain in a day – enough to make nearly a million loaves!

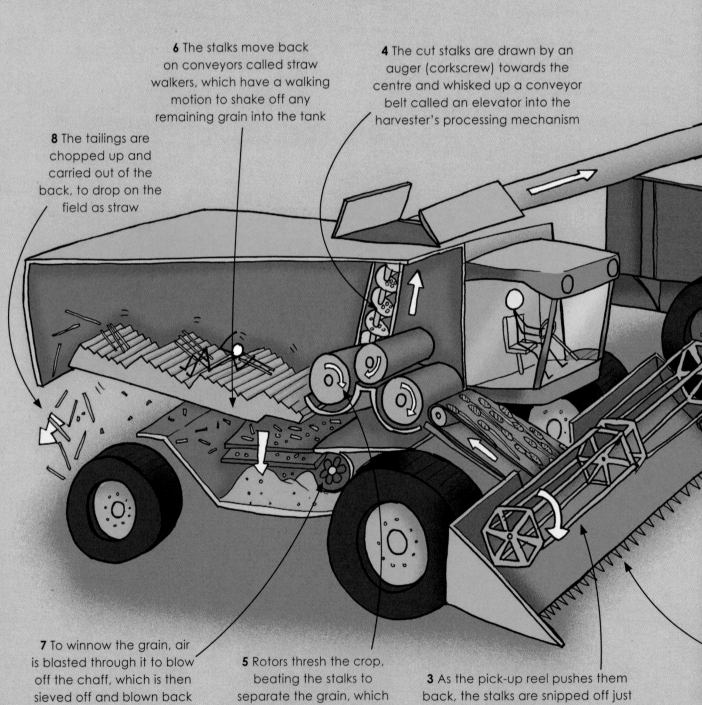

6 The stalks move back on conveyors called straw walkers, which have a walking motion to shake off any remaining grain into the tank

4 The cut stalks are drawn by an auger (corkscrew) towards the centre and whisked up a conveyor belt called an elevator into the harvester's processing mechanism

8 The tailings are chopped up and carried out of the back, to drop on the field as straw

7 To winnow the grain, air is blasted through it to blow off the chaff, which is then sieved off and blown back on to the field

5 Rotors thresh the crop, beating the stalks to separate the grain, which drops into a collecting tank

3 As the pick-up reel pushes them back, the stalks are snipped off just above the ground by the cutter bar

All-in-one harvesters

Combine harvesters get their name from combining all the tasks needed to gather wheat. As they drive through a field of ripe wheat or any other cereal crop, they cut the stalks, separate the grain, and clean and collect it automatically all in one go, using rotating blades, wheels, sieves, and conveyors. They combine the three main tasks in harvesting:

- Reaping – cutting and gathering the stalks

- Threshing – shaking or beating the stalks to loosen the grain from the 'tailings', the stalks that become straw

- Winnowing – getting rid of the scaly unwanted 'chaff', which holds the grain

Tiring work

Hefty farm machines have to cross soft earth and mud in all kinds of terrain and weather. So they have some of the biggest, chunkiest tyres in the world. The biggest tractor tyres are almost 2.7 m (9 ft) tall.

9 When the grain tank is full, the grain is carried up from the tank by an elevator and shoots out of a side pipe (sometimes called the unloader) into a waiting trailer.

2 The slowly rotating pick-up reel has teeth and bars called bats that push the stalks towards the cutter

1 The header gathers the stalks in at the front with a pair of sharp pincers called crop dividers

Semi-submersible Rigs

Some of the best sources of oil and natural gas lie below the seabed. To get at them, oil rig workers have to set up huge drilling platforms out at sea. But what if the water is too deep to rest the supports for the platform on the seabed? Then what's needed is a semi-submersible rig, which rests on pontoons (tanks) that float just under the surface of the sea.

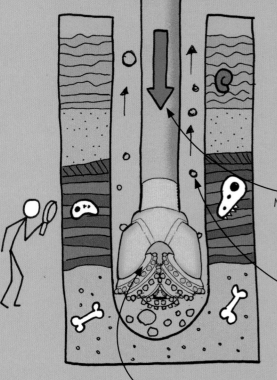

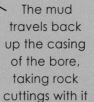

String time

The drill can reach 7,000 m (20,000 ft) into the seabed. Even under the sea, it could overheat when drilling into the solid rock of the seabed. So it is kept lubricated, cooled and cleaned by continuously pumping in a special fluid called drilling mud. The mud also brings the 'cuttings' (drilled rock fragments) up to the surface.

Mud is pumped down inside the drill 'string' – its entire length

The mud travels back up the casing of the bore, taking rock cuttings with it

A nozzle sprays mud on to the drill bit, cleaning the bit in the process

Tough bits

The head of the drill or 'drill bit' turns continuously and cuts slowly into the rock. Its cutting edges are toughened with different materials according to the rock type. Such materials include steel, tungsten-carbide, PDC (synthetic diamond) or even real diamond.

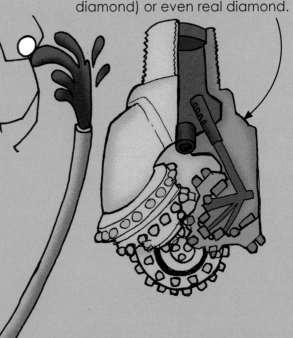

Gusher!

Once the hole has been drilled, the oil has to be extracted. So the rig workers reinforce the newly drilled hole with a casing of concrete. Next, they make little holes in the casing near the bottom to let oil in, and top the well with a 'Christmas tree' of control-valves. Finally, they send down acid or pressurized sand to break through the last layer of rock. The oil then gushes up through the pipe under its own pressure.

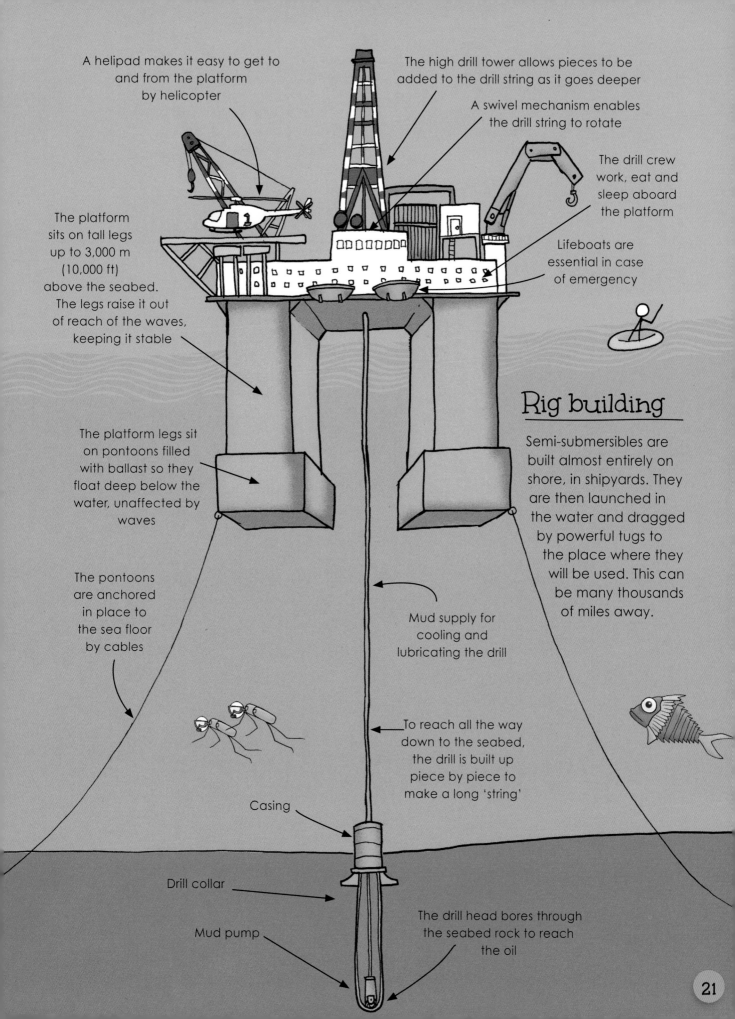

A helipad makes it easy to get to and from the platform by helicopter

The high drill tower allows pieces to be added to the drill string as it goes deeper

A swivel mechanism enables the drill string to rotate

The drill crew work, eat and sleep aboard the platform

The platform sits on tall legs up to 3,000 m (10,000 ft) above the seabed. The legs raise it out of reach of the waves, keeping it stable

Lifeboats are essential in case of emergency

Rig building

Semi-submersibles are built almost entirely on shore, in shipyards. They are then launched in the water and dragged by powerful tugs to the place where they will be used. This can be many thousands of miles away.

The platform legs sit on pontoons filled with ballast so they float deep below the water, unaffected by waves

The pontoons are anchored in place to the sea floor by cables

Mud supply for cooling and lubricating the drill

To reach all the way down to the seabed, the drill is built up piece by piece to make a long 'string'

Casing

Drill collar

Mud pump

The drill head bores through the seabed rock to reach the oil

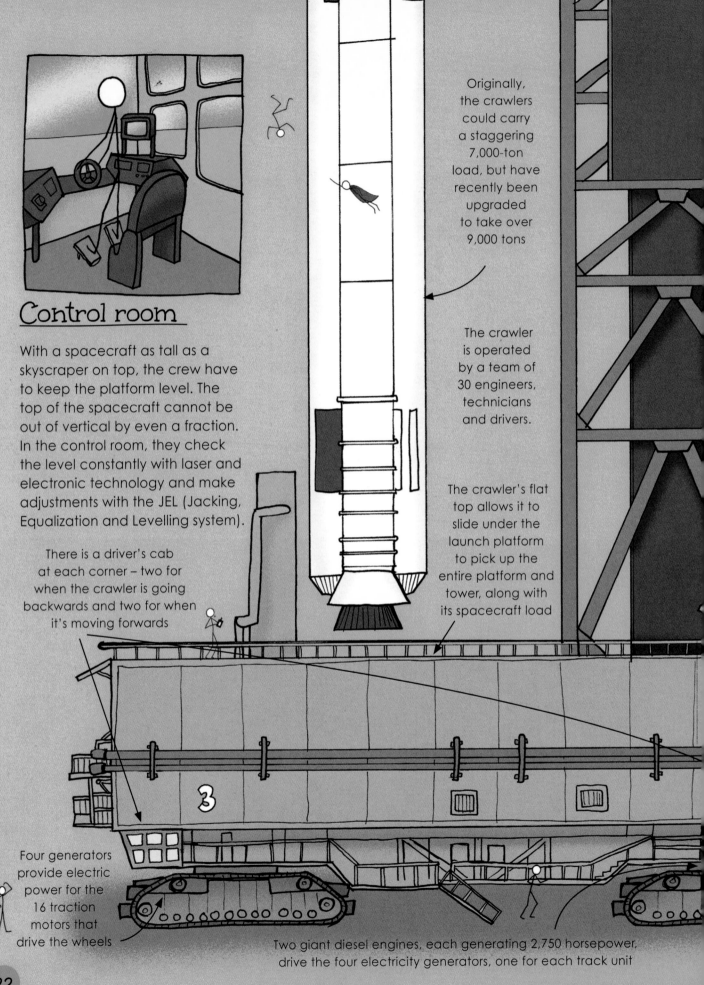

Control room

With a spacecraft as tall as a skyscraper on top, the crew have to keep the platform level. The top of the spacecraft cannot be out of vertical by even a fraction. In the control room, they check the level constantly with laser and electronic technology and make adjustments with the JEL (Jacking, Equalization and Levelling system).

There is a driver's cab at each corner – two for when the crawler is going backwards and two for when it's moving forwards

Originally, the crawlers could carry a staggering 7,000-ton load, but have recently been upgraded to take over 9,000 tons

The crawler is operated by a team of 30 engineers, technicians and drivers.

The crawler's flat top allows it to slide under the launch platform to pick up the entire platform and tower, along with its spacecraft load

Four generators provide electric power for the 16 traction motors that drive the wheels

Two giant diesel engines, each generating 2,750 horsepower, drive the four electricity generators, one for each track unit

Crawler Vehicles

Hans and Franz are the crawler vehicles used at the Kennedy Space Centre in the USA. Their task is to carry spacecraft from the buildings where they are assembled to the launchpads, ready to be blasted into space. They are the world's biggest self-propelled vehicles. Bucket Wheel Excavators may be bigger, but only Hans and Franz can move under their own power.

What do they carry?

- The crawlers were originally built to move the giant Saturn V rockets that carried the Apollo moon missions. That meant they were carrying a rocket that was 110 m (363 ft) tall, as well as its 121-m (398-ft) launch tower.

- After the Apollo missions finished, from 1979 the crawlers were reused for over 30 years to carry the Shuttles and their boosters into place for launch.

- Revamped, one crawler will take commercial rockets to the launchpad, while the other will carry the 97.5-m (320-ft) Space Launch System, designed to launch missions to Mars.

The crawlers are 40 m (131 ft) long and 34 m (113 ft) wide

The height of the crawler can be altered from 6 m (20 ft) to 8 m (26 ft)

Jacking cylinders can raise each side independently by up to 1.8 m (6 ft) to keep the platform completely level

The track units can swivel independently to steer the crawler.

The crawler runs on four track units, each with two tracks, and each powered by four electric motors.

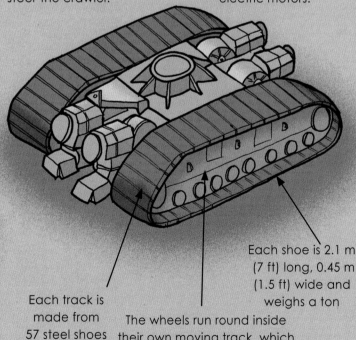

The crawlers can reach a speed of 1.6 km/h (1 mph) loaded and 3.2 km/h (2 mph) unloaded

The crawler weighs 2,750 tons without a load

Each track is made from 57 steel shoes

The wheels run round inside their own moving track, which spreads the load

Each shoe is 2.1 m (7 ft) long, 0.45 m (1.5 ft) wide and weighs a ton

Large Hadron Collider

The best way to find out what atoms are made of is to smash them together so they break apart. To do this, scientists build giant machines called particle accelerators in deep tunnels. Here, powerful magnets accelerate particles to huge speeds and hurl them together. The Large Hadron Collider (LHC) is the biggest.

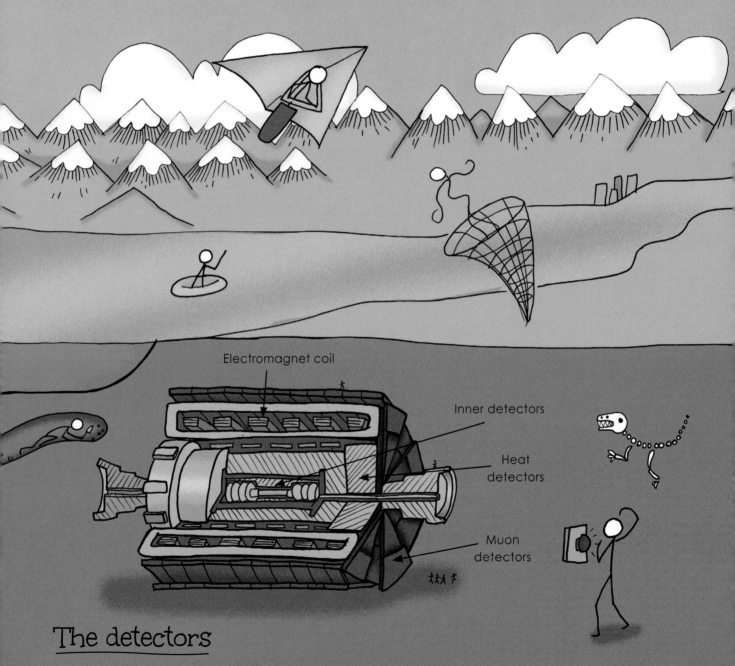

Electromagnet coil

Inner detectors

Heat detectors

Muon detectors

The detectors

Around the ring, there are six detectors where scientists can make observations and perform experiments. They are a bit like digital cameras. Although the particles they study are tiny, the detectors can be as much as three storeys high and weigh more than 5,000 tons. The biggest is ATLAS. It is so big and complicated it had to be taken underground in pieces and took five years to assemble. Its task is to detect collisions between protons.

Giant research project

The LHC is located deep underground on the border between Switzerland and France. It is run by CERN, the European Organization for Nuclear Research.

The Higgs Boson

The LHC has become famous for its hunt for a special particle called the Higgs Boson. It is this mysterious particle that scientists think may explain why things have mass – that is, why some things are light and others heavy. In 2013, they confirmed that they had seen it in the LHC, but no one knows quite what that means yet.

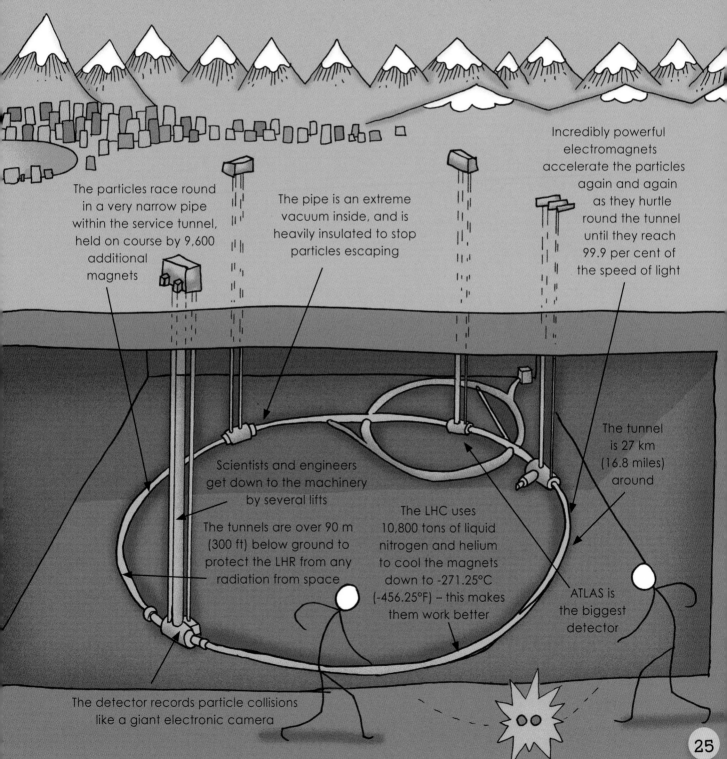

The particles race round in a very narrow pipe within the service tunnel, held on course by 9,600 additional magnets

The pipe is an extreme vacuum inside, and is heavily insulated to stop particles escaping

Incredibly powerful electromagnets accelerate the particles again and again as they hurtle round the tunnel until they reach 99.9 per cent of the speed of light

Scientists and engineers get down to the machinery by several lifts

The tunnels are over 90 m (300 ft) below ground to protect the LHR from any radiation from space

The LHC uses 10,800 tons of liquid nitrogen and helium to cool the magnets down to -271.25°C (-456.25°F) – this makes them work better

The tunnel is 27 km (16.8 miles) around

ATLAS is the biggest detector

The detector records particle collisions like a giant electronic camera

The top of the first hill is the highest point of the ride. So it has maximum potential energy. From this point, it can only go downhill... or can it?

Wheels all round

A roller coaster needs special wheels to hold it to the track as it roars from side to side and even goes right upside down. Ordinary train wheels can run only on top of the track. But roller-coaster wheels must run on top, along the side and underneath, too.

When you zoom down the slopes, you go into free fall and float off the seat, apparently weightless

As the cars hurtle faster and faster down the first slope, they gain kinetic energy – the energy of motion

After whizzing down the first hill, the cars have huge momentum. This means they are so loaded with kinetic energy they can bowl right up again – either high up another hill or right round in a loop

⇨ = acceleration

➡ = centrifugal force

⇨ = gravity

Loop the loop

As they loop, cars are held on to the track by the 'apparent force' created by the tug of war between gravity and the changing direction of their own acceleration. Loops on roller coasters have to be teardrop-shaped, not round, to keep the forces in balance.

Roller Coasters

Roller coasters might look like very mad trains. But these super-scary rides need no engine or power. They are driven by gravity and momentum alone. They only need power to launch them from the top of the first hill. After that, they just go and go...

Lift-off

On older roller coasters, the ride starts with a slow haul up the first, tallest hill (called the lift hill) by a chain that hooks into the base of the cars. As the train climbs higher, the further it has to fall, and the more potential energy it gains – the energy of gravity.

Whoosh!

Instead of the slow crawl up the lift hill, modern roller coasters start with a power launch that blasts you straight to high speeds, using electromagnets, hydraulics or compressed air. Within a few seconds of the start, you may be travelling at 160 km/h (100 mph)!

Shooting down the big loop, they gain enough kinetic energy to roar up the second loop. They've lost a bit of energy, though, so the second loop has to be smaller

Climbing to the top of the second loop gives another boost in potential energy – enough to make the cars accelerate again

The acceleration is just enough to give them the kinetic energy to climb the final slope, although friction and air resistance begin to slow them down

The cars are brought to a halt at the end by magnetic brakes

Older roller coasters have wooden tracks, but most modern tracks are tubes of steel that can be twisted into all kinds of shapes

Safety is vital on roller coasters, so riders are strapped or barred in securely before the ride.

Abrams Tank

Tanks are the most intimidating of all war machines, designed to blast their way across battlefields. They seem unstoppable with their huge weight, heavy armour and enormous firepower. They can be stopped, but it is not easy, which is why the 68-ton M1 Abrams tank is one of the US Army's key battlefield weapons.

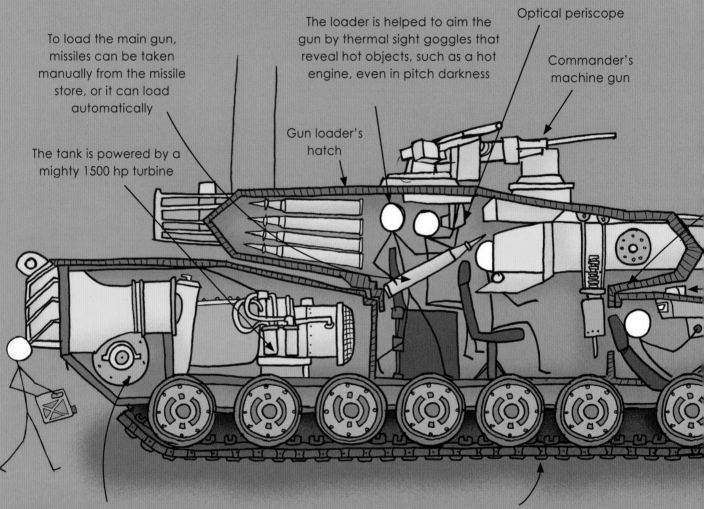

To load the main gun, missiles can be taken manually from the missile store, or it can load automatically

The tank is powered by a mighty 1500 hp turbine

The loader is helped to aim the gun by thermal sight goggles that reveal hot objects, such as a hot engine, even in pitch darkness

Optical periscope

Commander's machine gun

Gun loader's hatch

To protect the crew in case of a hit, the fuel and ammunition are stored in armoured compartments designed with blow-off panels that blow out away from the crew.

Tracks bear the tank's huge weight by spreading the load, and allow it to ride relentlessly over all kinds of terrain. The engine drives the wheels, which roll along the inside of the track, so that the track rolls forward.

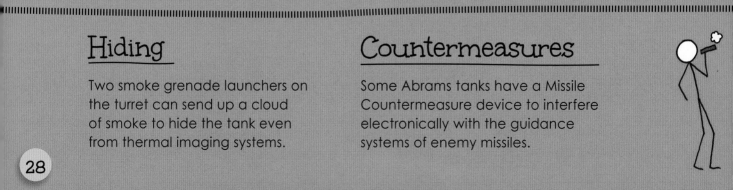

Hiding

Two smoke grenade launchers on the turret can send up a cloud of smoke to hide the tank even from thermal imaging systems.

Countermeasures

Some Abrams tanks have a Missile Countermeasure device to interfere electronically with the guidance systems of enemy missiles.

The driver

The tank driver slides in to lie back in the cramped space at the front of the tank, called the driver's station. There is no direct view out. Instead, he or she sees where to go through periscope views displayed on three screens.

Dials left to right: engine rev counter, speedometer, fuel gauge

Mission check

Damage warning lights

Left-hand track control

Right-hand track control

Engine power control

The gun turret swivels to aim the main gun in different directions

Driver's hatch

The main weapon is a 9.7-m (32.04-ft) M256A1 gun designed to destroy tanks, armoured vehicles and low-flying aircraft

Fire brigade
The tank has its own instant fire extinguishers, in case the interior ever catches fire.

The Abrams' armour plating is not just thick steel – it is a multi-layered shield of steel, ceramic, plastic and Kevlar that offers much greater protection by absorbing some of the shock

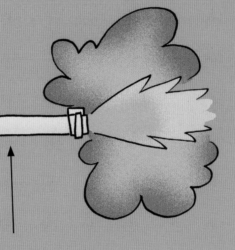

The front of the turret and hull get extra protection from a coating of very dense depleted uranium, which has the effect of a 0.6-m (2-ft) wall of steel

To make it harder to spot, the tank is painted a flat green in wooded and grassy areas, and tan in the desert

Strange Inventions

Intriguing giant machine designs date from the earliest times...

Magic doors

If you thought automatic doors were pretty modern, think again. Nearly 2,000 years ago, a mechanical genius called Hero, who lived in Alexandria in Egypt, invented a mechanism for opening the gigantic doors of Greek temples as if by magic. When the priests lit a fire on the altar, the hot air was used to move water, which then triggered an ingenious mechanism to move counterweights that swung the great doors open – and even blew hot air to create a blast on giant trumpets. No wonder visitors were awed.

Cosmic clock

Robots may seem like recent creations – but inventors have been designing automata (machines that work by themselves) for thousands of years. One of the biggest was the 'Cosmic Engine' of Chinese minister Su Sung. This was actually one of the first clocks. It was 9 m (30 ft) high and worked via rotating wheels and water pressure (or liquid mercury). At certain times of day, full-sized mechanical men and women at the top would ring bells and bash gongs. It ran for 30 years between 1092 and 1126CE.

Giant wood ant

It looks like a terrifying six-legged giant insect. In fact, the 'walking harvester' by Plustech/ Timberjack was the prototype for a real machine designed to help lumberjacks cut and gather trees in tricky terrain. The legs are moved in an ant-like way by computer, according to the driver's instructions. It has an antenna-like arm at the front for chopping down trees and picking them up.

Fountain machine

King Louis XIV of France wanted the world's biggest fountains to shoot water into the air at his palace at Versailles. So he commissioned the Marly Machine, finished in 1684. This huge pumping machine, with its 250 pumps, used an array of giant paddles to force water 152 m (500 ft) up from the River Seine to the palace gardens. It pumped as much water every day as was consumed by the entire population of Paris.

The world's biggest spider

In 2008, French company La Machine presented their giant mechanical spider – just for fun – at a parade in Liverpool, UK, as part of the city's celebrations as European capital of culture. The towering arachnid, nicknamed 'La Princesse', is 15 m (50 ft) tall and weighs 37 tons. It walks on eight legs with 50 hydraulically moved joints, and needs 12 people to operate it.

Glossary

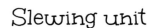

Cutterhead

The cutting face of a tunnel boring machine

Electromagnets

Powerful magnets activated by an electric current

Hadron

Any particle, such as protons and neutrons, made with a combination of quarks, the most basic particles of all

Haul truck

A giant dump truck used in mines and quarries

Hopper

An open container for loose bulk material that can be easily tipped or poured out

Hydraulic

Power system based on pushing fluids through tubes with pistons

Jib

The long arm that carries a crane's load

Kinetic energy

The energy something has because it is moving

Potential energy

The energy something has because of its position, typically its height above the ground

Reaping

Cutting and gathering the stalks when harvesting cereals

Submersible

A craft or machine designed to work underwater

Slewing unit

The turntable at the top of the crane tower that allows the jib to swivel

Threshing

Shaking or beating the stalks to loosen the grain when harvesting cereals

Torque

The turning force of an engine

Tower crane

A crane on a tall tower

Winnowing

Getting rid of scaly unwanted 'chaff', which holds the grain, when harvesting cereals

INDEX

The Author

John Farndon is Royal Literary Fellow at Anglia Ruskin University in Cambridge, UK. He has written numerous books for adults and children on science, technology and nature, and been shortlisted four times for the Royal Society's Young People's Book Prize. He has recently been creating science stories for children for the Moscow Polytech science festival.

The Illustrator

John Paul has a BSc in Biology from the University of Sussex, UK, and a graduate certificate in animation from the University of the West of England. He devotes his spare time to growing chilli pepper, perfecting his plan for a sustainable future and caring for a small plastic dinosaur. He has three pet squid that live in the bath, which makes drawing in ink quite economical …

Picture Credits (abbreviations: t = top; b = bottom; c = centre; l = left; r = right)
© www.shutterstock.com: 6 cr, 6 bl, 7 tr, 7cl, 7br, 8 bl, 8 br, 9 tl, 9 tr, 9 cr, 9 bl, 12 bc, 15 tl, 17 bl, 19 tl

9 br Olga Popova / Shutterstock.com, 23 tl Gary Blakeley / Shutterstock.com